THE BULL, THE MOON AND THE CORONET OF STARS

VAN BADHAM

CRURENCY PRESS
SYDNEY

GRIFFIN
THEATRE
COMPANY

CURRENCY PLAYS

First published in 2013
by Currency Press Pty Ltd,
PO Box 2287, Strawberry Hills, NSW, 2012, Australia
enquiries@currency.com.au
www.currency.com.au

in association with Griffin Theatre Company

National Library of Australia CIP data is available from the National Library of
Australia Catalogue: http://catalogue.nla.gov.au

Typeset by Claire Grady for Currency Press.
Cover photograph by Brett Boardman. Cover design by Interbrand.
Front cover shows Matt Zeremes and Silvia Colloca.

Currency Press acknowledges the Traditional Owners of the Country on which
we live and work. We pay our respects to all Aboriginal and Torres Strait
Islander Elders, past and present.

Contents

For Tom Holloway

The Bull, the Moon and the Coronet of Stars was first produced by Merrigong Theatre Company, Griffin Theatre Company and HotHouse Theatre at the Illawarra Performing Arts Centre, Wollongong, on 19 April 2012, with the following cast:

MICHAEL / MARK   Matt Zeremes

MARION   Silvia Colloca

Director, Lee Lewis
Designer, Anna Tregloan
Lighting Designer, Verity Hampson
Composer and Sound Designer, Steve Francis
Stage Manager, Karina McKenzie

ACKNOWLEDGEMENTS

The Bull, the Moon and the Coronet of Stars was originally conceived as *The Bull*, a short audio play commissioned by the Onassis Programme for the Pots and Plays Festival at the Ashmolean Museum, Oxford, UK, in 2011. *The Bull* was produced and directed by Helen Eastman and performed by Alice Barclay and Simon Muller, with sound design by Dan Gareh for York Street Studios. The playwright acknowledges the work of Helen Eastman, the Onassis Programme, the Ashmolean Museum, Jenni Medway, the Ashfield City Council Thirning Villa Artist-in-Residence programme and Playwriting Australia in the development of the expanded play, *The Bull, the Moon and the Coronet of Stars*. The playwright acknowledges, in this last instance, the generous work of Chris Mead, Susanna Dowling, Lucy Bell and Matt Zeremes in the play's dramaturgical adaptation for the stage. The playwright further recognises the crucial support provided by the stageplay's original producing partners, Merrigong Theatre Company, Griffin Theatre Company and Hothouse Theatre Company.

CHARACTERS

A MICHAEL, a publications officer at the Ashmolean Museum Oxford. 30s.

MARK, a sommelier in the restaurant of Portmeirion Village, Wales. 30s.

B MARION, a visual artist. 30s.

These are just suggestions. Lines can be assigned at directoral discretion.

SETTING

The Bull: The Ashmolean Museum, Oxford

The Moon: A train between Oxford and Bangor

The Coronet of Stars: Portmeirion tourist village, Wales

Present day.

A NOTE ON THE TEXT

When a backslash (/) occurs within the text, it indicates overlapping dialogue.

Italics within the text indicate that the line is mimetic from the performative character.

'Inverted commas' indicate that the line is mimetic from an external character.

All other lines are diegetic.

This play went to press before the end of rehearsals and may differ slightly from the play as performed.

PART I: THE BULL

The Ashmolean Museum, Oxford.

A: He didn't think much of her at first. His wife was a taller woman. Freckles and long legs and straight dark hair. Smaller breasts.

When Marion was brought into the museum office for the first time, the new artist-in-residence, he thought: *short*. Marion wore her light brown hair in plaits like a much younger woman, had glasses. *Short and fat*—and not his type. She'd been in the museum office a week, before she came in wearing the dress.

This is when he noticed Marion properly. The dress was blue, patterned with purple flowers. It clung to her. *Not plump*—he surprised himself—*ripe*. Later the same day, when he came into the photocopier room, Marion was leant over a paper tray, replacing some A4. He stood in the doorway—she didn't know he was there—she couldn't have known how much of her thighs were visible, the hem of her dress barely covered her arse. That was when it began.

A *and* B: The blue dress day.

B: He was attractive. Shaking his hand, her first day at the museum, she only barely suppressed the instinctive hatred that broiled within her. When she was twenty, she'd given her heart to an attractive man, and in return he'd given himself to her housemate, on a rug in the lounge room, when he thought she was soundly in bed. Amongst drinking and dancing, she'd had attractive men since and always loved them too quickly—a blond judge's associate who was far too young for her, a jealous sound engineer with fists like hams, a conceptual artist with long black hair and a beard and an opus made mostly of vanity. Her current boyfriend was balding and red-faced and lovely and they were living together now and it was comfortable.

A: *Michael.*

B: *Marion. Artist in residence.*

A: *Publications officer.*

B: *You do the museum guide—*

A: *And all the captioning. Press releases.*

Pause.

B: His hand was firm. That was when it began for her. He was tall and brown and his hair was a halo of brown and he wore glasses, too. Damn the sense of intimacy that comes from both wearing glasses. Broad shoulders. This was her first day there. The early sign of a paunch. It humanised him.

A: But—he was married.

B: Debbie the general manager told her he was married. His wife was some kind of teacher—and thin, and pretty. They'd married young. Expensive wedding. There was a photograph on his desk. Black and white. Wife in a white sheath.

A: If she felt something before the blue dress day, she kept it well hidden.

B: He was safe, she told herself, because he was married. They had found her a small glass office, with a computer, an empty desk and a drafting desk. It had glass walls and so did his office, across the hall from hers. She sketched a daily procession of objects they brought in for her—pots, and brooches, Roman keys, Saxon coins… relics of the ordered disorder that sprung a museum from what, four hundred years ago, had been a cabinet of curiosities.

A: Michael would glance at Marion through the glass.

B: She would carefully time her visits to the coffee room to be a minute after his. *Hi.*

A: *Hi.*

B: One day, she decided to wear the blue dress. It wasn't provocative. He was married.

A: The second incident involved a cake.

B: That was the night the windows were shattered.

A: It was Jenni the admin assistant's birthday. He didn't get too involved in these things. Drink coffee, smile, chew cake. Pretend to be interested. This was before the windows shattered.

B: Marion baked.

A: The most extraordinary perfume to this ordinary cake. He ate one slice, he ate another. The icing was thick and sweet. *Who made this?*

B: *I did. It's made with honey and lavender.*

A: *A woman of unusual taste—and many different talents.*

B: *These things have been said.*

A: *Yeah?* This is the pause in which he can choose not to speak, to chew on his cake, to be married. *These things have been said by whom?*

B: *Better men than you.* Why has she said this?

A: [*mouthful of cake*] *That's provocative.*

B: *You're licking cake off your fingers.*

A: *Yeah—*

B: *That's also provocative.*

A: He takes his cake back into his office.

B: She shouldn't have said anything.

A: He opens the document on his desktop—the monograph he has to edit on the new urn.

B: Stupid attractive men distract her—she says things she doesn't mean—he'll think she's a tramp, a slut, or desperate, or worse—she has a boyfriend and they live together—

A: He glances up over his computer. She's leaning over her desk, studying the corners of a broken terracotta plate.

B: What's worse than desperate?

A: Today she's wearing a V-neck shirt. He stares and stares at the round curves of her breasts.

B: That night, at the precise time he makes love to his wife—

A: Thinking how thin she is, how suddenly pale and brittle—

B: The glass breaks in the Museum windows.

A: The police came into the office the next day, followed by the maintenance men, the window fitters, the cleaners. Everyone has to announce to everyone there's been a break in—things have to be cleaned, things have to be assessed.

B: Nothing's missing—but no-one can work out how security glass could just break like that.

A: She's sketching the face of a particularly plump policeman. She thinks no-one else notices. 'The guards saw nothing, the alarm worked perfectly, it must have been kids—'

B: 'But how? But how?'

A: Her face reflects the deep seriousness of everyone else, but she's drawn a policeman with a head like a pig.

B: She offers to make herself useful and draw the broken glass.

A: And he notices, and they make eye contact.

B: And the shards of glass fell outside the windows, as if they'd been smashed from within.

A: And she smiles.

B: This will be the night that the guards hear footsteps on the ground— that are not footsteps—

A: She wears glasses and has plaits and she's short and round her hair is light brown gold and she's nothing like his wife—

B: They're hooves—the cloven hooves of an animal—

A: She's beautiful.

B: The next day. A kettle whistles. *Do I hear coffee being made?*

A: *The kettle boils for thee.*

B: *You're so chivalrous, Michael. Are you like this with everybody?*

A: *Do you really want me to tell you you're not special?*

B: *Of course I'm special. You're making me a coffee and I didn't even ask you to.*

A: *I saw the need in your eyes. It frightened me.*

B: *Everyone's frightened today. They think there's a demonic goat loose in the museum. Did you hear?*

A: *Marion—*

B: *Thank you—*

A: *What do you do here, exactly?*

B: *You know what I do, Michael. You watch me do it.*

A: *I've watched you draw a policeman who looks like a pig and a traumatised guard with the head of an ass.*

B: *And a publications officer like a wild, wild stallion.*

A: *Really?*

B: *No.*

A: *What are we paying you for?*

B: *Literally?*

A: *Literally.*

B: *Decoration.*

A: In bed, with his wife. She's sleeping, and her hair on his naked chest feels sticky. He rolls to his side, she presses her sticky face to his neck, her sticky chest to his back, her sticky thighs to the back of his legs. He can't stand it. He gets up, drinks a glass of water. Stands over the bed.

B: He swore an oath in church to cherish her. Marion sleeps next to a stonemason.

A: Objectively, his wife is exactly the same woman she was two weeks ago. Nose pointed, nature calm, hair dark, breasts small. He gets back into bed.

B: He has sworn before God to honour her. Marion. Stonemason.

A: Half-sleep. Restlessness. A dream—a nightmare—four horses tear a chariot through an orange sky—everything is the colour of burning confusion—black horses rear—stallions—he can't control the reins—the chariot flies—

B: Everything smells of smoke.

A: A fire in the museum. Electrical fault—but the firemen caught it in time.

B: They said the walls were wet with condensation.

A: He has to get a new office.

B: *Jesus, Michael… you look… terrible.*

A: He has to get a new job. One of the insurance assessors who came into the office today told the chief administrator there were scratch marks on a cabinet containing a Grecian urn. The guards have quit.

B: *It's not the business in the museum, is it? Is it getting to you? They're just noticing things that have been there forever because they're finally looking at them the right way.*

A: *I'm not sleeping very well.*

B: *Maybe your wife kicks.*

A: *What does your husband do?*

B: *In bed?*

    Pause.

  We're not married.

A: *Oh.*

B: *We live together. Three years.*

A: *That's practically married.*

B: *Then I'm sure you can imagine us in bed—*

    Very awkward pause.

  He's a sculptor.

A: *An artist?*

B: *A stonemason. He's small and tough and he doesn't say much.*

A: *Do you talk like this—together? [Beat.] Together do you talk like this?*

B: *No. He can form coherent sentences.*

A: *I like talking to you, Marion. It's the conversational equivalent of hunting big game.*

B: *A big game—?! / Game? / You're comparing me to a large ravenous boar? / The Erymanthian Boar/ The Cretan Bull?!*

A: */ Yeah / Yeah / That's not what I / No—No—No—that's not / what I—*

B: */ Some ravenous wild pig or / or / or—*

A: */ no / like a lion. I meant, like a lion.*

    Beat.

B: Marion's boyfriend is lovely and a stonemason and good at cooking and carpentry and not averse to children and they haven't had sex in more than a month. More than a month more than a month and she's a lion, she's got snakes in her hair, she's descended from swans, she's a three-headed dog—she tries to sketch pottery and she is the ocean, a shell, a pearl, who longs to be eaten by a sea monster—a weeping mother, pan pipes—the things she tries so desperately to draw—

A: There is a serious problem, now, regarding the guards.

B: Her whole world is two dimensional—a satyr, a sphinx—

A: Convinced there is a ghost in the museum, or a monster, they have quit.

B: Gods of wildness dance in the remnants of smashed crockery!

A: No guards will replace them. Rumours have spread. Stories of sightings around the museum. The lurking shadow of a monstrous bull.

B: She goes to the bathroom to wash her face. Debbie the General Manager is here. Crying. Guards won't guard the museum. The police will only police from outside. Thousands of priceless artifacts in a building where the walls sweat, the windows burst, electricity starts fires and something is wandering, wandering with cloven hoofs—

B *and* A: An emergency staff meeting is announced.

A: 'Who will guard the museum?'

B: Marion attends the emergency staff meeting. The Director, who she barely knows, is here. His face is lined, but he smiles.

A: 'The most frightening thing in the museum at the moment is insurance adjusters.'

B: This is his joke.

A: 'Without guards, the insurance is void. Without guards, the museum is an open candy house to thieves.'

B: 'We will have to guard', says the Director. 'It's voluntary. We'll take it in shifts. We're not afraid.'

A: Everyone's afraid. Debbie the General Manager cries. But Michael thinks of his wife.

B: So silent, the rumble of a plane overhead makes everyone shiver.

A: Her sticky hair, her bony hips, the hard bed, the chariot—

B: 'Who'll take the first shift?'

A: *I'll do it*, says Michael.

B: Heads turn, her heart leaps.

A: *The whole night. I'll be fine on my own. It's kids or a prankster— maybe it's the guards. But someone has to put an end to this.*

B: Before her, his shoulders broaden, his muscles swell. Behind his glasses, grey light glimmers. His mane of hair. Warrior. Champion.

A: *No, no, I'll be fine on my own. Just someone bring me some dinner.*

B: *I'll do it*, Marion says. *He likes my cake.*

   Pause.

A: A ticking clock. An empty hall. He's not a guard, so they've left the building fully-lit. He has a mobile phone, and the police are just outside. The air is cool. His wife has done nothing wrong. He has time to think. He wanders cabinet to cabinet.

B: Tick tick.

A: He wanders.

B: Tick tick.

A: His wife is beautiful.

B: Tick tick.

A: He thinks of the wedding photo, the white sheath. How it slid from her body in the beige light of the honeymoon suite. Her dark hair at her neck—he loves her, really. Tick goes the clock, tick the smear of the scratched glass. *What's caused this?* Closer he comes, sees the streak in the cabinet above head high. It catches the light. So does the surface of a pot. Two-dimensional man and bull. He's looking at a pot, when Marion appears.

A *and* B: Tick, tick, tock.

B: Three police have let her through the door. They're jokey and friendly and she gives them cupcakes like she's feeding Cerberus. Yap yap yap and she shivers as she crosses the threshold of the building.

A: Tick tick.

B: *Michael...!*

A: Tick tick.

B: *Michael...?*

A: He doesn't have to answer. This could be a great revenge on her conversational barbs, her glasses, her plump lips. Being ignored. Her blue dress. The mistake he makes is to wonder what she's wearing.

B: *Michael... I brought cake...*

A: *Here*, he croaks. *Here, among the Greeks.*

B: There is nothing sinful in this, she says to herself. He is safe because he is married and he is doing something dangerous and she is merely bringing cake. And she will offer him cake and his mouth will be full of her but it will not be sinful. The cake is really an offering, through him, to a god...

She just doesn't know which one.

A: She's wearing a long belted coat. *Is it cold?* He says, because he is suddenly warm.

B: She just holds out a Tupperware box full of cupcakes.

A: *Thanks.*

B: He takes the box.

A: *Can't really eat these standing up.*

B: *Not a lot of dining tables.*

A: *We have the floor.*

B: *Are you asking me to join you?*

A: *Will you?*

B: *If you ask.*

A *and* B: He just sits.

A *and* B: She just sits.

A: She leans over as she peels open the box. The thick scent of lavender and honey. It's dizzying.

B: She unbelts her trench coat. It's suddenly warm.

A: He puts a cake in his mouth, watching her fingers on the silver buckle. The mid button of the coat. The button at the chest. The lower button. Chews. Watches her slide one arm out of her coat. The next arm. She's wearing the blue dress. Purple flowers on her chest, side, stomach—the discarded coat's lined with polka dots, the fabric has a soft sheen.

B: *It's silk—*

A: She says, stroking the fabric of the lining of her coat, spreading it under her hand—

B: *You can touch it.*

A: One hand on the silky fabric, the other pressing a cake into his mouth. *You going to eat something?*

B: Her stomach's full of butterflies—and dragonflies, and bees. She doesn't know where to put her hands.

A: He gobbles a cake. Did he hear something?

B: A flicker on her face. She's heard it, too.

A: *It's the cops outside.*

B: *Playing tricks. Freaking us out.*

A: *Maybe it's the Director. Maybe this is a weird corporate team building exercise.*

B: *Except I'm not corporate and there is no team. Just you and me.*

A: *You should eat.*

B: It's transgression to eat from what you offer to a god—but she doesn't say this out loud.

A: He snatches his forgotten hand from the silk lining on the floor.

B: There's another sound. Distant. Like a grunt. *A car, it must be.*

A: *You have to eat something.*

B: *No—*

A: *Is there poison in this cake?*

B: *Yeah.* Breathing too heavily. *I'm a necrophiliac, it's a come on.*

A: *Let you in on a secret—*

B: He says, scooping up another cupcake—

A: *I'm a necrophiliac, too.*

B: *No!*

A: He forces the cake against her laughing mouth.

B: *He's a boy, a youth, a teenager! You're a big teenager!*

A: She falls backwards onto the coat. *Teenager?! Teenager?!* Forcing the cake into her—his fingers press against her lips as she swallows—

B: Again, he snatches his hand away.

A: As if they were never in their thirties, that they were teenagers, that he wasn't married—

B: Laughing, laughing—no boyfriend, no sex, the great god Pan—

A: Heart beating. And it hasn't—

B: Not like this—

A: For so long.

> *Pause.*

B: She reassembles herself from the floor.

A: *It's like a purring, that sound in the distance.*

B: *It's a machine or something. A carburettor, outside.*

A: *What's in your bag?*

B: *I thought if you wanted me to stay—*

A: *If you want me to want you to stay—*

B: *If you wanted some company...*

A: She rattles a box from her bag, flips open a sketchbook.

B: *I thought I could draw you. Or it. Whatever it is.*

A: *A carburettor. Can you draw a carburettor?*

B: *I'm artist in residence, I can draw anything. I am the vehicle of a powerful muse. As are you.*

A: *The muse of press releases.* Her pen on the empty page.

B: *The muse of captioning.*

A: Scratch goes the pen on the paper. A shriek in the distance.

B: Something animal. *We're just freaking ourselves out now.*

A: *Do I stay still?*

B: *Stay perfectly still.*

A: His body does, but his eyes do not. They slide from her shoulders, down the blue waterfall of her dress, to her naked knees. The sketchbook rests on them like a guardian, casting shadow.

B: She can't properly follow the line of his body. His lungs pump too much air. He thinks he's sitting still but he heaves and falls—

A: Footsteps—

B: Heaves and falls—

A: His eyes in the triangle of shadow between her knees on the floor, her naked knees on silk, on the floor—

B: Can she hear footsteps?

A: And she's only a metre away from him—less—

B: *Michael, I can hear footsteps. They're inside.*

A: The sketchbook slides away. She leans back to look for the source of the noise and the hem of her dress disappears into the edge of skin at the top of her thigh—

B: *It's coming closer! Do we wait? Do we go to it?*

A: The meat of her thigh—her hands skim over it, pushing her dress over it.

B: Closer—closer and closer—

A: And the lights go out. They're blind.

B: *Michael? Michael—are you here?*

A: *Yes.*

B: *Where?*

A: *Here.* The noise has stopped. The footsteps. *Where is it?*

B: *Touch me. I'm frightened.*

A: Electrical fault. It must be. *What's causing this?*

B: The smell of walking sweat—

A: The walls—it must be the air-conditioning, or—what sounds like footsteps, hoovesteps—

B: On her tongue, the taste of sweat on meat, on hair, on hide, on horn—

A: *It's a generator winding down—or a change of temperature causing the floor to crack, or the cabinets—*

B: *Will you touch me?*

A: He feels her fear in the air around her, the smell and taste of meat and sweat and lavender—*I have to find my phone. Call the cops. We can't be left like this.*

B: But he can't find his phone. He touches the floor.

A: Feels a handful of silk.

B: His hands run over the floor like frantic spiders, searching for his phone. They run over her ankle—she shrieks—

A: *Sorry—*

B: They run over her knee—

A: His first contact with her skin—he slaps his hand on the floor—*Look for yours, and you can call mine—and we'll have light—*

B: The black is absolute dark, we are two shadows that only have fingers, feet, knees and spines.

A: The scent of meat in his nostrils—*Where is it?!*

B: *I can't find my bag.*

A: *You had it a second ago.*

B: *It wasn't pitch black a second ago. I don't want to get lost in this—*

A: *I'm right here!*

B: *I don't want to crash through a glass cabinet—Grab the edge of my coat—I'll grab the other—I'll do a search, you anchor me.*

A *and* B: The smell of animal hair and honey.

A: She wheels around him, clutching the coat—

B: The tension of fabric between them—*I can't find it—*

A: *My foot hit something—*

B: *My art supplies. Squat—I'll come down to you—don't let go—!*

A: And on the floor, one hand grabs the rattling box, and with the other he pulls the coat, and with it, her—

B: And their hands meet—

A: Warmth. Ignition—he can't see it coming—he can't dodge it—

B: She flings herself into his arms, her arms clinch his neck / and her body's slammed against him—

A: / And her body's slammed against him—chest to chest and pressed so tight that to steady himself / he has to hold her—

B: / He has to hold her, he's the only solid thing in the darkness, they're on their knees, / ribcage against ribcage—

A: / Ribcage against ribcage and their clothes, his skin, hers—

B: It's just membrane, a thin tissue of membrane—

A: Her heart thumps against his chest, and he holds her more tightly— *Are you frightened?* His hair in her hair—

B: The rungs of her spine amongst his fingers—

A: Her face against his / face—

B: / *Michael—*

A: *Marion*—her heart beats through his skin as if he is already inside her—

B: *Listen…*
    Listen—
    It's here—!

A: Nothing but breath—nothing but her breath and his breath and her breath and his breath—and the breath—/ the breath—

B: / The breath of an animal.

A: [*whispering*] *Is it in this room? Is it coming for us?*

B: [*whispering*] *I don't know.*

A: An unnatural sound. A gargled roar—the inhalation of steam through its own nostrils—metres away—

B: And she knew in this moment—clutched in the dark—

A *and* B: He would die for her.

A: *I have to know what it is.*

B: The animal breathes, machine breath, the breath of a slow locomotive.

A: *Stay here!*

B: *But what if it's dangerous?*

A: *If it's dangerous, the worst thing we could do is be frightened. I'll deal with it—*

B: *I'll come with you—/ I don't want you to get hurt—*

A: */ I don't want you to get hurt. It's probably just a loose animal—*

B: *Hold my hand.*

A: *I'm going to need two hands—just in case—*

B: *In case—/ what?!*

A: */ If we could be—be tied, or if we had something—*

B: She rattles the box of pens. *String. Give me your hand. I'm tying string around your wrist.*

A: *Crouch under a cabinet and you should be safe—*

B: *This is me at the end of the spool.*

A: *But if it comes to you, pull the string—and I'll find you—I'll find you, Marion—*

B: And his hands are sure in the dark—

A: They find her face—

B: And her eyes close—

A: There is an animal loose in the museum—

B: He kisses her face—

A: Just her face—

B *and* A: The lightest kiss—

B: The gentlest kiss—

A: I have done nothing wrong—

B: And he steps away. Into the darkness—

A: Into the void that hides the animal. Slow / steps—

B: / Slow steps—

A: And the / echo of steps—

B: / The echo of steps.

A: Two / sounds—

B: / Two—

A: The unwinding string—

B: And the animal at the edge of the dark—her heart's beating like mad—

A: His whole body is a cage of bees—his lips sting from contact with her cheeks—

B: And that growl, in the dark, the steaming breath—

A: Closer closer further / further closer closer—

B: / The unwinding string—

A: Around a corner, towards it—the dankness, the darkness, the smell—

B: She feels it unspool in her hands—always the temptation—

A: The desire—

B: To tug on the string, give the false signal that will have him wind back to her—

A: For his lips to meet her mouth this time / For her soft lips, her mouth filled with lavender.

B: / For her soft lips, her mouth filled with lavender.

A: And he hears the heartbeat of this third thing—

B: The animal in the dark—

A: It's taller than he is—he senses it—

B: And she does—its dark shadow radiates in the dark—a projection of heat, and it's seven feet high—

A: This vast thing, moving through the darkness—can it see? His leg hits something—

B: String—she feels a tug—does that mean—? *Is that a signal?*

A: He bounces back against the string, retraces his steps, hunting this thing, the seven-foot darkness—

B: And she stands, silently moves through the lightlessness, pulling herself along the string.

A: The thread is loose behind him.

B: A snort.

B *and* A: It's closer than they think.
　　　　It's in the room.

B: *What's / it waiting for?*

A: / *What's it waiting for?*

B: She can feel it.

A: He can feel it.

A *and* B: Without seeing it. Beyond seven feet tall. Towering horns. The chest and arms of a man.

B: The creature born of adultery.

A: The offence of transgression.

B: Neck and head of a bull.

A: Its head turns—he feels the sharp passage of its horns, slicing the air—

B: They are both silent but the Minotaur's heartbeat pumps through the room like a bass.

B: She opens her arms / steps forward / she tells the creature / *If I am the offering that can save his life / let it be /* the pulse of its heart / she floats towards it / on the rhythm of it / she takes its wet muzzle in her hands / she is all gentleness / she licks the Minotaur's face / worms her tongue between its lips / woman to bull / the second act is the act of reversal / her hands slide to its horns / gripping them, she licks again / and licks its chops / its bull's head / licks / the Minotaur licks back / the arms around her are a man's / licks / the bull chops / its horns dip / licks / the Minotaur seizes her wrists with its man's arms, she holds its head / licks / hands in the fabric of her blue dress / the Minotaur's man hands are hot on the backs of her thighs / seizes / licks / seizes / fabric torn from her body / the Minotaur / seizes and grabs / the hands of a man and her own hands clenching the horns / let it be a man / let it be a man / the animal is a bull / the man / the animal / the bull that brings her to the ground / hands full of her flesh and it parts her / the bull / the floor / thighs of a man / licks / tastes / heaves / gives / it is wrapped in her / hips of a man / she is an offering of herself and she has brought it down / the bull's head / the licks / the seizes / the bull the man the bull the man the bull the man the bull the man the bull / open and full she's full she's man bull man / she's full / she's full—!

A: / He raises his hands / steps forward / this is the shadow of threat / the risk of the hurt / it moves / he ducks first / jabs / it's too quick / he's missed it / and shock—the thing has him by the face / its hands / its hands have come for his neck and its twisting / its bull face in his own face he's twisting / the wetness of the animal / its muzzle over his as it tightens his grip on its head / lick / the smell of meat and lavender / flings his hands at its horns, to wrestle the bull's neck / it bucks! / jab / twists / he grips one hand at its leg / this wetness on his face / the Minotaur gurgles / he shoves / the taste of meat and he vaults open the creature's thigh / twists / the thing buckles at its neck, its wetness in his face again / the thigh springs! The thing falls! / they've fallen to the floor, the wrestle is here / he pins the thing by its horns / pressing his body on top of it / his weight on it / twists / buckles / twists / he has it pinned! / Its buckling thighs under his thighs / chest pressed by his chest / it wriggles it squirms / twists / the horns / the arms flails / he has wrestled the Minotaur to the floor / too quick to be caught by its arms / its grip on its horns / too strong / it's pressed to the floor / it bucks it bucks it bucks it bucks he tastes blood / it struggles / it bucks and he slams himself into it and a slam and a slam and a slam and it heaves and he heaves the last expense of his draining strength as it heaves, slows, stops, breathes, sleeps and perishes... perishes.

B: And amongst the limbs of the spent creature, she curled her limbs amongst the Minotaur, and she slept.

A: And exhausted, he slept.

B: And she nuzzled the Minotaur, and thought how much like a man it was.

A: He was the first to open his eyes. The streaming light poured through the window, warming him awake. He sat up, thinking the shape next to him was the strangled carcass of the Minotaur.

B: It was not.

A: Michael gasped. He was on the floor of the museum. Around his wrist was tied a red thread—and the red thread ran through the room—around cabinets like a lasso, around stands and pillars for exhibits, and it pooled in a puddle where he lay.

B: On an open trench coat, his skin against its silken lining, where he'd slept. Next to her.

A: Next to the round, soft, beautiful curves of her naked body. The woman—he knows it—he knows—he has sunk his flesh into, and enjoyed.

A *and* B: The woman who is not his wife.

B: She sighs.

A: He reaches for his glasses, first—then the discarded rags of his underwear, his shirt, his trousers. He dresses, looking at her, sketching in his mind the lines of her, the curves of her body. The unwound plaits of her golden hair. He slips into his shoes. This is the best way. It is the only way. He does not kiss her goodbye.

B: The Minotaur will not return to the museum.

A: He pockets only an uneaten cupcake from the Tupperware box, and he eats it as he walks away, and out the door.

B: She has been dreaming of lions, and bulls, and wrestling. Marion has dreamt of the great god Pan, and the greater Poseidon, lord of the sea, and her body has been an ocean and rolled and heaved like a tide. She rolls and heaves, into the beam of the sunlight. It wakes her. Her eyes flutter open to the white sand of a beach. Seabirds fly through a blue sky. She sits up.

A: And Ariadne, who helped Theseus slay the Minotaur, awakes alone, and abandoned, on the island of Naxos.

END OF PART I

PART II: THE MOON

This takes place on the stage, between the two human performers standing on it. A's character is clearly differentiated from the part he has just played. He is changing his costume or demeanor from MICHAEL *to* MARK.

B *drinks water to refresh herself. She is broken-hearted and perhaps she collapses to the ground.*

B: *I've got an interesting and varied career. I could do with more money but I'm not doing badly. I'm in good health. Honestly, I think this is the best I've ever looked.*

> *After some seconds,* B *erupts with an horrific gasp. Maybe she cries.*

> *How did I get here?*

A: She's on a train.

B: *I have packed a suitcase, I have boarded a train.*

> *Sensing—if not fully comprehending—how broken she is,* A *approaches* B.

A: *Did you ever see him again?*

B: *The wages of sin are death. The wages of adultery are waking alone in a museum—*

A: *Or on a beach—*

B: *Sand is the wreckage of sea. Museums are the wreckage of civilisations. The king of media releases didn't even leave me a note.*

A: 'Dear Marion—'

B: My skin stank of him.

A: 'Sometimes a connection between people is a perfect encapsulation because events are both momentous and brief.'

B: I could smell saliva from his mouth in my hair.

A: 'I won't call you. I won't email. I'll disappear into my marriage like the king who left his lover on the island of Naxos / sailing a ship with black sails back to his city of Athens.'

B: / Sailing a ship with black sails back to his city of Athens.'
    'With love—?'

A: [*shaking his head to correct her*] 'Michael.'

B: The wages of adultery are waking alone and feeling like death. I hate every cell of my flesh and every strand of my hair. Fuck. Fuck—it was stupid, it was childish, it was pointless, but—
I loved him.

In silence, A [*the actor, the performer*] *comes closer to her...*

A: *Look at it as a character development opportunity—*
B: *What?!*
A: *Without pain, we don't exist—*
B: *I think I can exist without pain.*
A: *Without people hurting one another, there's no such thing as story. There's no such thing as history. The entire record of human myth and achievement is a catalogue of the cruelties we visit on each other.*
B: *This is not an historical situation! This is me on the floor with my heart broken!*
A: *Ariadne, on a beach, with her heart broken.*
B: *But my—name—is—Marion.*

MICHAEL *has now completely transformed into* MARK.

Marion's empty house.

A: This is Marion's empty house.
B: 'Your life is not over when your heart is broken. Just one version of your life.'
A: This is what the books said.
B: Books Marion bought by the bucket load. Pails and downloaded pails of self-help e-books—
A: *Swim Amongst the Swans, Dance Among the Divas, Sex and the Supremacy of Self, Women Who Run with the Wolves, Women Who Love Too Much, Women-who-women-who—*
B: If her Kindle were a bookshelf, it would've groaned.
A: But she had no bookshelves now. And no house either.
B: This is no longer Marion's house.
A: There is no longer a sculptor boyfriend—
B: He may have been able to make dragons from rock and temples from stone—
A: But he couldn't make anything of his girlfriend's tearful confession of infidelity on the floor of a Museum—

B: With a ball of twine, an invisible publications officer / and a spectral *bloody bull.*

A: / And a spectral *bloody bull.*

B: What Marion did have, when she left Oxford, was the first job she could find as far away as possible—

A: And a grey plastic suitcase carrying a wardrobe suitable for a Welsh autumn—

B: And in her grey suitcase, a velvet pouch preserving the two golden braids she had shorn from her head.

A *and* B: Marion cut off her hair.

B: *Short. Like a nun, oh hairdresser. Cropped and penitent.*

A: Each golden curl cut away, only silver bristles remained.

B: She binned her makeup—

A: She burned her blue dress.

B: It was autumn.

A: Her autumn.

B: Now both thirty-five and a thousand years old—

A: Marion boards a train from Oxford, England to Bangor, Wales.

B: Sailing past the window is a dull white sky, trees bright with orange and slow dying—

A: Black mountains, thick with coal.

B: In the train, silver-haired Marion stares at the weathered sinew of her hands as her fingers weave the crescent of a white moon into a tapestry on her lap.

A: The train races like a cloud towards Marion's grey new horizon.

B: She wears shapeless grey trousers.

A: Hides her breasts in a shapeless grey shirt—and whispers to her tapestry:

B: *The sunlight is out in me. I'm done with men and sex and bulls and lust and a wet tongue. These colourless lips will kiss nothing—I sew a banner to my new gods in the sky, the chaste women of the moon.*

A: Marion's train enters a tunnel.

B: And because she's looking at the reflection of her face in the sudden mirrors of the train windows, thinking how ancient she looks, how sexless—

A: Marion doesn't notice—that the moon in her lap is laughing.

END OF PART II

PART III: THE CORONET OF STARS

A: Mark's mistake, that dim Welsh morning—

B: Dim *mid*-morning—

A: Was to welcome the Drawing Club Ladies to the hotel with champagne.

B: Marion is the new art tutor at a resort on the coast of Snowdonia.

A: The resort comprises a seaside hotel and Italianate village with rentable cottages—a beach—a pool—an esplanade—a moored boat—a grotto mosaic of oyster shells—a piazza with pillars and statues—a Japanese bridge, dog cemetery and temple— an eccentric architect's bricolage of facades salvaged from the shattered colonnades of World War Two Europe…

B: Marion crosses water as her cab approaches the resort via a one-lane bridge… She's dispatched at twin pink tollgates, and wanders cobblestone spiral streets into clumps of pastel buildings. Their eaves gather round the skirt of the sky like the strange edges of a dream… She floats past the sea and the white hotel as she's guided to her lodgings in a shoreside cottage with a tower—

A: There are some restaurants and several gift shops… and—Mark! The Australian sommelier in charge this autumn, of fine wining, with dining—*Greetings, ladies—'nother top-up?*

B: Usually, the Drawing Club Ladies are presented with handmade Welsh chocolates to enhance their stay in the Hotel.

A: But Mark, promoted to hotel promotions promoter, given that it's the off-season and the only guests are the Drawing Club…

B: Mark has a more *interpretative approach* to hospitality.

A: And an awesome hangover… He was only thinking about what his Mum might enjoy.

B: A demi-bottle each of a fizzy pink sparkling that he accidentally over-ordered for a wedding, each placed on the Ladies' identical blue and white bureaus in near identical blue and white rooms. With a compliments slip.

A: He printed the bloody compliments slips himself. And supervised Lucy when he got her to fold them all.

B: Marion appears at the reception desk and is *not* complimentary.

A: Maria tells Mark the short-haired, grey-garbed old crone howled in her face.

B: / [*to* MARIA] *The Ladies have turned up to the first day of my autumn art residential drunk and giggly and I haven't been able to complete the induction—!*

A: / [*mimicking*] 'The Ladies have turned up to the first day of her autumn art residential drunk and giggly and she hasn't been able to complete her induction—!'

A: She's so cross that Maria and Lucy have to persuade her to stand outside to inhale some calming sea air.

B: It's sundown and the sky is the colour of a dying tree.

A: Women are the only thing Mark knows more about than wine and as he walks outside he's already got a measure of this vicious hag, just from her silhouette—Short hair, and glasses.

B: Marion grips the rail that runs along the concrete esplanade.

A: Women with glasses are always judgmental bitches.

B: For a couple of seconds she forgets she's angry—

A: Her shirt's like a grey tent over her body, her trousers make her hipless—

B: She stares at the orange, afternoon sea.

A: You do alright with dykes, Mark tells himself. Talk plain. When she looks up, maintain eye contact.

B: She turns—

A: *Are you the art teacher?*

B: Shielding her eyes from the glare of the sun—she can't see him—

A: Her face as fierce as he guessed, her hair as spiky as a personal threat—

B: *Whose brilliant idea was the sparkling fucking rosé? You've got twenty-two uninsured old ladies wandering the premises, pissed as newts.*

A: *Madam, I apologise that you weren't consulted before there was a provision of alcohol to your students—*

B: She still can't see him and the sound of his voice causes a tremble of fear in her heart.

A: Something about her face is out of place—

B: It has the timbre of an attractive man—!

A: *I take full responsibility, and will compensate you for any inconvenience caused.*

B: It has the tremor of an attractive man!

A: Glasses, check, sneer, check, rounded cheek, short hair, yes, / yes—

B: / No, Marion begs heaven, no—spare me from his kind.

A: *Your eyebrows—!*

B: *My what?!*

A: Art-hag has eyebrows with arcs as precise as the bow of Eros.

B: She lets herself see the eyes of the brown young man who does *not* wear glasses.

A: No butch dyke has ever had eyebrows like that.

B: The sommelier is small and knobbly with a crooked leg and a scalpful of dark, sandy cowlick curls—

A: Why is the crazy bitch smiling?

B: He's not handsome at all!

A: *If you are dining in the hotel restaurant this evening, I should like to provide you with wines from my personal cellar to complement your meal—*

B: *I don't enjoy wine. And I'll be taking this up with your line manager.*

A: And she walks away—elated.

B: Not handsome at all!

A: *Who the hell doesn't enjoy wine?*

B: He's still asking himself this, and Lucy this, and Maria this, and Rolf the fat chef this—when Marion and the Drawing Club Ladies enter the dining room at precisely seven o'clock to take their dinner.

A: *Lucy, give Cranky Skinbird a glass of the Henri Favre.*

B: The Ladies are impressed, their teacher's status raised by the sommelier's act of hospitality.

A: But Marion says:

B: *No.*

A: *Then give her a glass of the Mumm.*

B: But Marion says: no.

A: *A bottle of the Pol Roger.*

B: Which Marion collectivises with her table, to the delighted squeals of grey-haired rich-men's widows, as Marion herself says: / no.

A: / No. Mark actually glares at her. He knows about women and he knows about wine and with wine, he can open all women—

B: But this one. She sees him glaring—

A: And that's when—

B: The cork of the Pol Roger / shoots from the neck in shocked Lucy's hands—

A: / Shoots from the neck in shocked Lucy's hands—smacking into the chandelier overhead with a crystalline crash—

B: The Ladies shriek—

A: Amongst the racket of glass, his eyes don't move from hers. He's seen it now. Something in her that's in him, too.

B: Marion's residence is not in the village, it's at the resort's southernmost point. She asks for harder pillows. She's slightly disappointed the blankets on her bed aren't scratchy.

A: Mark has availed himself of the hotel's Olympus Suite—

B: The boss is away—

A: But here are Maria and Lucy—

B: It's midnight, and Marion's already been asleep for two hours. She dreams—

A: That Maria and Lucy are at the foot of Mark's king-size bed, kissing one another.

B: Touching in the way that girls who aren't lesbians try to convince straight men that they are lesbians. And in the dream—

A: Mark watches them, back to the headboard, his listless hand holding a full glass of wine. His naked chest doesn't sweat. Two girls kiss.

B: Mark's grown horns and is wearing a wreath of snakes around his head. And the two waitresses from the restaurant shake out their hair and say: 'Come on, what's wrong?'

A: Lucy stops kissing Maria and, grumpy, folds her arms across her breasts.

B: They stare at Mark.

A: *Nothing. Nothing's wrong.*

B: But it takes him longer than it ever has, to put down his glass, and join in.

A: The very second Mark's hand touches Maria—

B: Marion wakes in her bed and she doesn't know why and she doesn't manage to get back to sleep.

A: The Drawing Club Ladies are also having strange dreams.

B: They tell this to Marion during their morning drawing class in the hotel conservatory. Marion has thoughtfully arranged a still life composition consisting of a harlequin mask, a drum, a pinecone and some wax grapes.

A: 'You look so tired, Marion.'

B: *The pillow I sleep on isn't hard enough—*

A: 'Must be all that secret dancing you're doing.'

B: *I don't dance. Take a charcoal.*

A: 'In my dream last night, and in Miriam's, too. And in Emma's. And Audrina's. All of us dreamt you were dancing barefoot in a grove of walnut trees, a drum beating and ivy in your hair. Have you ever thought of growing your hair out, Marion?'

B: *No, I haven't. Take a charcoal.*

A: Every day, the same coldness from her—the ice-armour that protects whatever her secret is. Mark sees her in the restaurant, waves—

B: There are no waves on the moon.

A: Encounters the drawing class on the grassy Piazza, sketching the sculptures and the fountain. The ladies chatter around him. But she—

B: There is no grass on the moon.

A: *And her drawings aren't even that interesting.* He sneaks into the conservatory between her lessons and peeks through the teacher's desk. Always, a still life. Drums and cymbals that will never make music. A perfectly executed dead fig.

B: It's autumn, and even at the resort, the trees are dying.

A: Before the week ends, Mark decides that Marion's behaviour is a personal insult.

B: For dinner that evening, Rolf the fat chef has roasted some turkey.

A: Perfectly roasted pink flesh from a fresh, juicy bird and with it, of course, a brilliant white burgundy.

B: As she has every night, Marion sips at a soda water.

A: *Which is, frankly, not on—*

B: Mark says this to Lucy, even as he scrutinises every bubble in the glass at Marion's lips.

A: *You can't tell me these women are here because Welsh light is better for drawing. This is an off-season package designed around indoor activity—that, is the consumption of fine food and wine.*

B: 'Yes, Mark.'

A: *She's just challenging my status—some act of pathetic retribution because half-bottles of cut-price rosé showed her students more of a good time than she can.*

B: 'Yes, Mark.'

A: *Right. If that's what she wants.*

B: Marion has a fork between her teeth when she first hears the drums. She's been thinking about Michael—for the eighth time in a minute. She's grateful for the distraction of heavy bass vibrations through her feet—although they remind her of dancing, they at least return her glassy eyes from a dead-end reverie to the room—where old women are standing, chairs are moving and linen serviettes flutter like birds.

Music.

A: *DJ Dark Mark the Night Prowler at the decks! Liberate your inner leopards, lovely ladies—time to get beastly with the Beastie Boys.*

The Beastie Boys' 'Do It' plays.

B: *What—the—fuck—?* Her ladies are—her ladies—

A: [*rapping*] *'Well, I'm a lion-skinned lover when I sway my tail,*
    Got paws, horns an' claws and I'm a twice-born male—
    I'm the beast that want's to nail ya, but I ain't no gaoler—
    I'm a wild-ass motherfucker, I'll fuck yo' better than a
        sailor—!'

B: The sandy-haired sommelier is waving his arms in the air, and the waitresses are next to him *whipping their hair*—he's behind a deck and there's a dance floor—

A: And it's heaving—!

B: And a group of women who she knows have an average age of seventy are *shaking it* to the beat of a song she hasn't heard since 1999.

A: *Rock it old school—or just rock it old!*

B: Resin beads bounce against breasts as they bump and shimmy—she's the only person still sitting at a table—it's too much—She's going to speak to him, this could be unsafe. *This is not a safe activity.*

A: *Aw, come on. Dancing's good for the heart.*

B: *At your age perhaps, not at theirs. Turn off the music. Turn it off—these women will be getting stress fractures—!*

A: *Lady, the only stress fracture 'round this place is you.*

B: *I beg your pardon?!*

A: *Walking around with a carrot up your arse. Soda water with dinner. Bed before ten. Still life drawing.* Too *frightened to even wave at someone in case whatever it is you don't want people to know leaps out of your armpit—maybe it wouldn't be such a big problem if you took five minutes to have a dance and chill the fuck out.*

B: *I don't need to chill—I'm as cold as the FROZEN FUCKING MOON OF EUROPA and I am telling you to—telling you—*

A: And that's when she sees what Mark's smiling at.

B: At the corner of the dance floor, Audrina and Esme from the Drawing Club—

A: Both seventy-two, very drunk and sweaty with dancing—are *getting it on.* With tongues.

B: *Jesus Christ.*

A: And she's gone.

B: Marion doesn't even go back for her coat. She pushes through the restaurant doors, she's in the hallway, she's on the front steps, she's halfway back to her isolated cottage and the cold night air of a cold Welsh autumn means nothing—her cheeks are burning, her scalp is burning, her hands are in claws, she hates this, she hates him, she hates Wales, she hates Michael, she hates herself and she hates the stupid vessel of her adulterous body and a sudden, overweening desire to be swallowed by darkness takes over and she veers from the path home to a path into the woods.

A: She doesn't know that Mark is following her—and *he* doesn't know *why* he's following her—

B: She stumbles into the black thicket of a solid embankment—

A: He only knows that if she catches him, he'll just turn himself into a goat and run away.

B: Thrusting forward with a crunch crunch across grass and rocks / and bramble.

A: / He is the shadow man, the night prowler, he makes no noise as he follows.

B: And burning Marion pushes through black branches until her feet tread on something crunchily different sounding and here she's in / a clearing.

A: / Moonlight illumes the dome of the tiny marble temple hidden in the woods.

B: She staggers up its steps, inside and then collapses to its cold floor amongst dust and dusty leaves and dust. She looks up, and knows this is where she has come to, and why.

A: Above her head, a strip of skylight.

B: And through that skylight, / the moon—

A: / The moon—waxing as full as a pregnant belly. (I saw her face light up like the temple dome, marble and smooth. I watched her whisper a prayer.)

B: And then Marion, weary with rage—

A: Mark sees this, from his corner of shadow—

B: Marion exhausted by the demands of her broken heart and the shame of love spent in so many wrong directions—

A: He comes in to the temple, where Marion lies curled in a pool of still moonlight.

B: Marion is overwhelmed by coldness and the moon, and passes out.

A: *Marion?*

> *Pause.*

> *You alright in there?*

> *No response.*

He collects her cold limbs in his arms, and feels her heart beating. She's a lot lighter than he expected.

B: Marion's head rolls into his shoulder.

A: Like a lover's would.

B: And Mark carries her through thicket and bramble, carries her down the cement esplanade to her isolated cottage—

A: The furthest from the village—

B: The one on the shoreside with white walls and a tower.

A: Uses his skeleton key to let himself in to her white-walled room—

B: Ports Marion to her bed—

A: And is amazed— / how gently Hard Marion sinks into the mattress.

B: / How gently Hard Marion sinks into the mattress.

A: He takes off her glasses, holds them in his hand.

B: Her eyelashes tremble.

A: This close to her—

B: She is sailing across a blue sea—

A: Her lips are not hard—they're soft and full.

B: She's in a ship with black sails—

A: Her body curls into the bed, / like a lover's would.

B: / Like a lover's would… and the black-sailed ship reaches an island—

A: Her breasts float on the air of her breath—

B: She disembarks—and watches the ship sail away—

A: This is a body that has known and given love, cocooned in sexlessness to hide—what secret?

B: *Stay—stay here now—*

A: And this is what Mark knows—a woman, a bed, a request for his company, oh yes. He strokes her lip with his thumb, leans over her body on the bed—

B: *Don't leave with the ship, Michael—*

A: *Michael?!*

    A pause.

    [*Shrugging*] *Okay, 'Michael', whatever—*

B: *I cut the red thread from my wrist but it's still caught—*

A: She grabs his hand.

B: *Who's here?*

A: Her eyes flicker open and look at his face—

B: *Mark?*

A: But she's still dreaming—

B: *Mark, it's caught, it's still caught—the ship sailed away but even on this island, even here—whenever the moon passes behind a cloud— whenever it's dark, the bull roams, Mark…*

A: Clutching his hand—

B: *It roams, it's still wandering—*

A: Actually crushing it—

B: *Don't leave me to the bull*, she says.

A: And it's all… a bit—

B: *Mark—!*

A: Intimate.

B: *Please, don't leave me.*

A: Settles her head on the pillow. *I won't*, he says,

B: But he does.

A: Panic—and release! The door shuts behind him, the night air is bracing!

B: And now Marion dreams that Mark leaves her cottage, and gallops along the esplanade until he reaches the steps of the Hotel.

A: From the shadows emerges a trail of smoke, leading to a cigarette.

B: It's Emma, from the Drawing Club, silver hair around her shoulders. 'We missed you in there.'

A: *I was concerned for your tutor.*

B: 'A shame she ran out. She could use a good dance.'

A: *She could use a good fuck.*

B: 'Oh.' [*Pause.*] 'Couldn't we all?'

A: Women are what Mark knows more about than wine—

B: In Marion's dream, Mark takes the smoking septuagenarian on the stairs by the hand.

A: Leads her into his suite.

B: Kisses her nicotine mouth.

A: Peels away the layers of Emma's purple-winged blouse, her purple pantaloons, her flat shoes.

B: Leads Old Emma naked to his bed by a leash of the resin beads at her throat.

A: He uncorks a half-drunk bottle of cabernet sauvignon and he pours it over her shoulders.

B: Emma giggles.

A: Rivulets of red run over her nipples, over her stomach and thighs—

B: And pool in the grey thatch of pubic hair, as Emma opens her legs—

A: Mark sups on vintage as he makes love to Emma's mature flesh with his mouth.

B: What Marion couldn't possibly know—

A: Is that Mark is dreaming, too—of Marion's lips—

B: *Please, don't leave me.*

A: The old woman shudders out her first orgasm in years on Mark's tongue—

B: And Marion wakes, and thinks:

A *and* B: *How did I get here?*

B: When Marion arrives—early—for her drawing class the next morning, she's surprised to see her whole class already assembled, pads on their laps—

A: Class has already started, but it's not Marion's.

B: Mark, the ridiculous sommelier, is perched naked on a table and the women are drawing him.

A: *Good morning.*

B: Knobbly, stupid Mark with one knee up like a posing Olympian, probably thinking he's very sexy.

A: *The ladies expressed an interest in life drawing.*

B: *Most generous of you to volunteer, but you mustn't let us distract you from all the bottle-corking you have to do.*

A: *Oh, that was handled last night—*

B: Emma titters at the back of the room.

A: *But if you'd prefer me to leave—*

B: Of course, the ladies murmur complaint.

A: And Mark reaches for his towel—

B: *No. Stay—*

A: Squeals of delight, but he didn't expect this—

B: *This adds an interesting dimension to our work on texture.*

A: Marion approaches Emma—and hands the old woman a large paper bag—

B: *Emma, would you kindly place the bag over Mark's head. Now—*

A: The crinkle and smell of dark thick paper surrounds him.

B: *Choose whatever pose is comfortable, Mark. Everyone, you'll be drawing Mark paying particular attention to the qualities of the bag.*

A: Blind Mark swings his legs over the table because he'll be here for a while.

B: Marion does not pick up her sketchbook.

A: Bag or not, she'd have to be looking at him.

B: In her room is an old satchel she doesn't touch, containing an old sketchbook she doesn't touch, containing an old drawing of him. Of Michael, on the floor of the museum.

A: Mark is a naked man on a table—she'd have to be looking at him—

B: She will not touch or draw men again. She masks a sigh as she sits, casts her eyes around the room, the focused attention of the women drawing—already, their best work.

A: Look at me…

B: Sorts through her pencil case, cleans up some pastels…

A: Look at me… Look at me…

B: Glances out the window.

A: Jesus, Marion—!

B: And then she lets herself look, just once, at the headless naked man on the table.

A: A glance so intense, he can feel it.

B: *Uh!*

A: Did she say that out loud?

B: Did they really all hear it?

A: A grunt! A sexual grunt!

B: This shouldn't be happening. Sweat at her forehead, on the backs of her hands. The ladies rumble, the pads on their laps bob as they look at her, as she tries to cover her grunt with a cough, like an idiot. She's an idiot, he's an idiot, how did that happen?

A: She looks again!

B: Mark doesn't move so maybe he didn't hear. Maybe he just sat there with his shoulders broad and the hair across his chest the colour of a lion's fur, strength in his paws, horns sprouting from his scalp under the paper bag—the hot, hard, handsome man curves of his handsome man body on show now she's undistracted by the wild mess of his head. Sweat running down her neck—*Excuse me—*

A: Ha!

B: *I'm not feeling well—sorry, Ladies—*

A: She'll be his before midnight—

B: The rumble and ache in the pit of her stomach. *I need to get to the bathroom, Ladies, please—*

A: Open on his bed, her sweetmeats under his fingers, her tongue swollen with wine. He'll seduce her at dinner, she'll have come by dessert!

B: The conservatory door swings, but Marion—*excuse me, Audrina—* Marion doesn't—*please, can I—*limbs—paws—sweat—stomach— Mark—Jesus—*PLEASE—!*

A: *Can someone tell me what's going on?*

B: The acrid taste before her stomach gives way and—

A: *Oh, wow—*

B: Marion barely gets her hand over her mouth and—

A: *Did she make it through the door?*

B: A sweaty, swaying stagger down the hallway, into the bathroom off the foyer and thank God she makes the cubicle in time.

A: *Get Lucy—tell her to bring Marion some fresh water and a towel—*

B: Always, this constant war with her own flesh—

A: *Poor Marion.*

B: [*to heaven*] I DON'T HAVE ANY MORE HAIR TO CUT OFF.

A: Once she's back in her cottage, she phones the desk and tells Lucy she isn't well.

B: She doesn't make it to dinner.

A: Rolf the fat chef serves an entrée of oysters, and Mark's in such a vile mood that he treats all the Drawing Club Ladies to more pink champagne.

B: Marion spends an hour in the shower, scrubbing her skin with handfuls of salt.

A: Mark's at the turntables again—the drunken women make boisterous demands for wild dancing—

B: There's a thump thump thump of music on the breeze, emanating from the hotel.

A: Music pounds, but Mark's heart's not even in it when during a song he ducks into the storeroom to bang Maria against some cases of shiraz.

B: Marion dons a blue dressing gown, and locates the old satchel, the old sketchbook.

A: Back at the decks, the women are shaking and howling, drinking wine from the bottle—they've got Rolf on the dance floor, they've ripped off his shirt—

B: She can't resist one last glance at the drawing.

A: Mark's had an idea—

B: Her fingers on the creamy paper remember Michael's skin against hers on the museum floor.

A: *Toga party!*

B: She wraps the sketchbook in plastic, shoves on some boots and a scarf.

A: The women take to the linen tablecloths like big cats tearing at prey. They weave the plastic vine leaves used for table decoration into the curls of their grey hair. Rolf is stripped naked—

B: Marion begins a lonely pilgrimage from the cottage—

A: And they're dancing in a wild procession, red wine running at their mouths like blood—

B: The sketchbook is under her arm—

A: *Drums! Everyone grab a drum! Use a saucepan and a spoon, a bottle and a fork—we've got millions of them—*wine everywhere, drums, everywhere, Rolf's bouncing pink belly—

B: Along the esplanade, towards the moored boat.

A: Such a great banging that the timber in the floors and the glass in the chandeliers join in. They wheel Mark into their conga line and they paw him forward, through the doors—these women are roaring, pictures shake on the wall and every piece of cutlery in the kitchen goes jump.

B: Down the stone steps by the boat, and onto the sand.

A: Out of the restaurant, and into the hall, licking Rolf, licking him, licking Maria and Lucy, dancing, wine spilling, the women's teeth are sharp in their shining mouths, their fingernails are bent like claws, their skins ripple with spotted fur—

B: She hears the percussion at the open hotel doors, so she treads softly across the wet sand of low tide in the dark.

A: *To the beach!* Mew the ladies. *To the beach!* Cat-calls and miaows!

B: Marion reaches the water's edge, feels the tide lap at her boots.

A: Laughter as wine is spat, robes are torn, Miriam is biting Rolf the fat chef, Lucy is topless, Maria is pantsless—the procession shambles down the stone steps and Esme crashes giggling to the sand. She lands on her four feet and buckles, shedding her toga, her whiskers taut, her tail flicking into the air—

B: And Marion's too preoccupied with this final ritual of separation to hear—

A: *Cats—hey, cats, cats, cats, cats, cats—Is that—is that Marion?* Ladies are leopards, are a wild chariot that drives him to the edge of the water—*Shh—shh!* A pride of ears flash to his whispers— [*Whispering*] *It's Marion!*

B: She lowers the sketchbook into the water, and launches it from her hands.

A: *Shh—sneak up, sneak up, we'll push her in—Shhhh!*

B: It floats in a flicker of moonlight on water... and Marion's heart hurts so much, she yearns to start drowning.

A: *I'll push her—I'll do it—Shhh!*

B: But his hand just touches her shoulder—

A: All his leopards and panthers rear in a great, joyous roar around him—

B: Her scarf and robe swirl in a sudden wind—

A: Stars.

B: Sand.

A: Water.

B: And night sky.

A: This woman—

B: This man—

A: This frozen moment of her red scarf—

B: *How is the beach covered in... panthers?*

A: But his big cats have vanished. Leopards melt into sand, panthers to shadow.

A *and* B: Leaving Mark alone with Marion.

B: And his hand still on her shoulder.

>   *Pause.*

A: *Wow—wind's really pushing the clouds away. So many stars—*

B: *Why are you here?*

A: *Uh—I was going to push you in—*

B: She flicks away his hand and turns back to the sea, to the floating book that lingers by the shore.

A: *Come on, we were just fooling around—*

B: *You're in my face every five minutes—*

A: *And you've been rude to me since you arrived—*

B: *I've been professional. Is it so unusual for women to not throw themselves at you that it seems ungenerous when one keeps her pants on?*

A: *It is pretty unusual.*

B: Oh, he can't resist a smile—

A: *But you did grunt out loud when you saw me naked today.*

B: *And then I had to throw up.*

>   *Beat.*

A: The wind howls on the water.

>   *Silence.*

B: *I can't believe you had sex with Emma.*

A: *She's an adult.*

B: *She's certainly a lot more than just an adult.*

A: *And why are you down here by yourself in the middle of the night?*

    Beat.

B: The wind howls on the water.

    Silence.

A: *What's the book?*

B: *An old story that is long finished.*

A: *A story about a man?*

B: And here, the fissure in the surface of the cold moon: *A story about a very unavailable man.*

A: Intimacy—intimacy—

B: The moon cracks—

A: Hurtling towards him like an asteroid—

B: A great shudder in the night sky—

A: *Did you always know that he was married?*

B: Marion's head collapses into her hands.

A: *So, because you don't have a guy you already knew you couldn't have, you—what—shaved your head, swore off sex and ran away with old ladies—That's it? That's the bee up your arse?*

B: *Leave me alone.*

    Beat.

A: *He must've been magic in the sack.*

B: *It's all you think about—*

A: *It's all it could be—*

B: *I loved him. Loved him. It was stupid, but I fell in love with him and he left and now I'm—I'm this—I'm a remnant of getting it wrong. Do you understand?! Has it even happened to you?*

A: The wind howls and something is howling in Mark, too. *I don't know. I guess not.*

B: Cracking moon—

A: Falling asteroid—

B: Marion cries.

A: Or is she laughing?

B: Her red scarf whips in the wind. It hits Mark's chest.

A: He catches the scarf, winds it carefully back around Marion's neck.

B: His fingers graze her cheek. She blushes.

A: He blushes at her blush.

B: *My cheeks are sticky.*

A: *Here—come here—*

B: Marion sinks into Mark's shoulders and he wraps his arms around her.

A: In the wind, on the beach, is when Mark learns the secret that Marion doesn't even know she's keeping.

B: This woman is no priestess of the moon.

A: Mark feels through her skin the piece of sun that reveals her heritage as a granddaughter of the sky's fiery charioteer, the god of sunlight. Mark leans his head into hers and it's so warm.

B: The throb of his heart against her chest awakens… a slow throb in hers. The growing throb in her blood, limbs, lips and groin. *What's happening?*

A: And Mark, who has known sex without intimacy and passion without love, watches an intimate smile spread on his true love's face. *Marion—?!*

B: Her hair is growing.

A: Tendrils of gold streaked with silver tumble from her scalp, ooze between his fingers—

B: Curls slap into the water at their feet—

A: A fountain of hair overwhelms her head and shoulders, a silky river overflowing in his hands.

B: Her curls are heavy in the water—they're dragging her into the sea—*Help me—Mark—*

A: The unstoppable flood of hair—the tide trying to yank her from his arms—

B: *Help me!*

A: And with no other thought than to save her, the god Dionysius—

B: It's not much of a secret that Mark is Dionysius—

A: Dionysius plucks from the heaven above them a star from the Corona Borealis and uses the star to pin up a lock of her hair—

B: Another star to pin another lock, and another and another, so her hair will stop growing—

A: *You okay?*

B: Every star of the Corona, until Marion's hair is out of the water and the woman he loves wears a dazzling crown. [*Pause*] *Did we kiss then?*

> *He shakes his head.*

A: He walks her back to her cottage.

B: And she welcomes him in to the white-walled room.

A: *I'll fetch some scissors.*

B: He cuts the stars from Marion's hair and throws a new constellation into the sky from her bedroom window.

A: He throws the cut hair out, too—the strands transform into a flock of flying golden cranes.

B: Her remaining hair is long enough for her to plait two new braids.

A: And the cranes soar past them, and past the white egg of the full moon. *Did we kiss then?*

> *She shakes her head.*

B: Marion walked to her bed.

A: *It's pretty late. I guess I'd better go.*

B: And here Marion, who has always loved in the wrong direction, sees her right destination in a bashful flicker of Mark's eyes. *Come on— we both know you're staying here.*

A: *Just to sleep.*

B: *Yeah. Just to sleep.*

A: In the bed, in one another's arms—

B: The most vivid of dreams—

A: In his, she agrees to meet him the next day.

B: In hers, he shows her the secret vineyard where he's trying to grow his own wine.

A: Dreams merge / and flow—

B: / Where she meets him the day after that. And / the day after that—

A: / Where the Drawing Club Ladies pack up their pastels and leave, but she stays behind.

B: Where he has a word to his boss, and they both move into her cottage as caretakers for the winter.

A: *And then they woke up.*

B: *And then it was morning.*

A: They say there was only ever one faithful marriage in heaven.

B: And who would have thought that orgiastic Dionysius, god of wine and wildness, dancing, trancing, the ecstatic and insane—

A: Would happily be that bridegroom, and that Ariadne—

B: Marion—

A: Marion, would be the bride.

B: Marion, granddaughter of the sun—

A: Who helped Theseus slay the Minotaur—

B: Who got lost in a museum but found her way out again.

A: Marion, who once got dumped by a king—

B: But went on to pick up a god.

> *They look at one another.*

> *They share a first kiss.*

> *They look at one another.*

> *They share a second kiss.*

> *Blackout.*

THE END

Griffin Theatre Company, HotHouse Theatre and
Merrigong Theatre Company present the World Premiere of

THE BULL, THE MOON AND THE CORONET OF STARS
BY VAN BADHAM

Merrigong Theatre Company,
Illawarra Performing Arts Centre
17 - 27 April

Griffin Theatre Company,
SBW Stables Theatre
2 May - 8 June

HotHouse Theatre,
The Butter Factory Theatre
13 - 22 June

The Bull, The Moon and the Coronet of Stars was first
performed at Merrigong Theatre Company, Illawarra
Performing Arts Centre, Wollongong, 19 April 2013.

Director
Lee Lewis

Designer
Anna Tregloan

Lighting Designer
Verity Hampson

Composer and Sound Designer
Steve Francis

Stage Manager
Karina McKenzie

With
Matt Zeremes and Silvia Colloca

G T C
R H O
I E M
F A P
F T A
I R N
N E Y

Co Producers

merrigong
THEATRE CO

HotHouse
THEATRE

Government Sponsors

NSW
GOVERNMENT | Trade &
Investment
Arts NSW

Australian Government

Griffin Production Sponsor

nabprivatewealth nab

PLAYWRIGHT'S NOTE

My first summer in Melbourne was one that involved my body curled into beige carpet, tear-stained cheeks and a heaviness in my limbs I could not shift.

I had taken my dream job as the Artistic Associate at the Malthouse Theatre. I had discovered a beautiful Art Deco apartment in Melbourne's decorous CBD… and I had realised that my black-haired, British boyfriend would not be following me from London, after all.

I sobbed. Howled. Spent entire afternoons listening to all of Fleetwood Mac's *Rumours* on repeat, eating Nutella out of the jar.

Other evenings were spent with Tom Holloway - my fellow playwright and himself recently out of a relationship. We stomped around Melbourne together, being hurt. We indulged crankiness at the theatre. We gorged on Chinese food in late-night restaurants.

I was weepy; he, angry. This was an inversion - Tom is known for work of a tender nature: loving couples facing death, the aftermath of tragedy. Me, I'm known for political plays with the plots of action movies, guns and bombs.

I suggested Tom write a revenge comedy. He suggested I revisit a short-play I had written (when my relationship was dying) about adultery; he wanted to know how its characters may have survived the debris of misplaced affection.

This is the blessing of friendships between writers. I *did* go home and think about *The Bull*. Then, when director Matt Lutton asked me to recommend a playwright for an adaptation of *Dance of Death* - a brutal play about dysfunctional marriage - I knew who had that kind of anger to burn…

A year later, my heart has reknit over the process of writing *The Bull, the Moon and the Coronet of Stars*. I can also vouch that *Dance of Death* is hilariously vicious and Tom is throwing parties without Fleetwood Mac in earshot.

So, this, my romance of missteps, mistakes and the aches of complication, is, in truth, a love letter. It records that two playwrights once forgot love's joys but in time regained them. It celebrates the vocational alchemy of theatre-making, that transforms all pain into blessing.

And it's a devotion to Tom Holloway - whose friendship means more to me than the words of any mere love letter could express.

Van Badham

DIRECTOR'S NOTE

I'm sitting at the airport waiting for the flight that will take me to Albury to begin rehearsals for *The Bull, the Moon, and the Coronet of Stars*. We call it *The Bull* in the office because despite the gorgeousness of the full title, the office moves at such a pace that we don't have time to revel in the glory of the string of words Van has created. But that is exactly what I hope the production will do - make us take the time to revel in the journey through incredibly evocative language towards a hopeful vision of life.

I cannot thank Van enough for giving us a play that is essentially hopeful. In complex times playwrights critique us, provoke us and haunt us with observations of our worst selves. But sometimes... they very generously remind us that there is joy and light and humour. This is a precious play filled with these qualities. That a playwright as smart and cynical as Van is so selflessly willing to detail the vulnerability and self-doubt we all share in the realm of love makes us deeply indebted to her.

Here's to a playwright unafraid to create a work embracing the possibilities of the heart! Here's to future Griffin/HotHwouse/Merrigong partnerships! Here's to a vision of the world which reminds us that love can be at the centre! Here's to revelling in it!

Lee Lewis

Van Badham
Playwright

Van Badham is a playwright, novelist, screenwriter, critic, social commentator, broadcaster, dramaturg, director and cabaret performer. She has been called 'a major talent' by *The Guardian*, 'the brilliant Australian playwright' by *The Independent* and 'one of the leading voices of her generation' by *TimeOut London*. Van was based in London for ten years; here, her achievements included winning the NSDF International Play Script Competition and *Sunday Times* Harold Hobson Award for Drama Criticism, selection for the Summer Play Festival New York and national tours of her work supported by the Arts Council UK. She received commissions from Nabokov, Floodtide, LAMDA, Oxford Playhouse, the Royal Court and the BBC, and trained in writing for television on attachment with *Holby City*. From 2009–2011, Van was Literary Manager of the Finborough Theatre, London. In 2011, Van returned to her native Australia to take up an appointment to her present position as Artistic Associate (Writing) at Melbourne's Malthouse Theatre. In Australia, she has been selected for three National Play Festivals, won a Premier's Award for her play *Black Hands / Dead Section* and won numerous other national honours and awards for playwriting and screenwriting. Presently, she is completing the second volume in the three-book *Book of the Witch* novel saga for Pan Macmillan Australia. She writes occasional columns for many publications and in 2011 was co-host of a literary program for ABC radio. Internationally, Van's work has been staged in the USA, Germany, Austria, Iceland, Slovenia and Switzerland, and her 2011 play, *How It Is Or As You Like It* was staged at the Rijkstheater, Stockholm, Sweden in August 2012. Van is on twitter @vanbadham, and more information is available on her website at www.vanbadham.com.

Lee Lewis
Director
Lee is one of the Australia's leading directors, having worked for numerous main stage companies, including Sydney Theatre Company (*Honour, ZEBRA!* and *Love Lies Bleeding*), Belvoir (*That Face*), Bell Shakespeare (*Twelfth Night, The School for Wives*), and Griffin (*A Hoax, Silent Disco, The Call* and *The Nightwatchman*). Lee's most recent directing work includes *This Heaven* opening at Belvoir in February, and *Highway of Lost Hearts* for Darwin Festival. In 2013, Lewis will direct David Williamson's *Rupert* for Melbourne Theatre Company, and Van Badham's *The Bull, the Moon and the Coronet of Stars* for Griffin. Lee trained as an actor at Columbia University in the United States, working on Broadway and Off-Broadway productions, before returning to Australia to study directing at NIDA.

Anna Tregloan
Designer
Anna is a designer of staging and costumes for contemporary theatre, dance, film and circus, an installation artist and director. Her work has toured to all Australian capitals along with work showing in Edinburgh, Paris, New York, Prague, London, Kyoto, Malaysia, Belgium, Dublin, Holland and many other international stages. She has been privileged to receive several state and national awards including Helpmann and Green Room Awards, the John Truscott Award for Excellence in Design for Theatre and in 2010 an Australia Council Theatre Fellowship. She has worked with Sydney Theatre Company, Bell Shakespeare Company, Ranter's Theatre, Playbox, Legs on the Wall, Force Majeure, Arena Theatre Company, Melbourne Workers' Theatre, I.C.E., Back to Back, Danceworks, Handspan, Chunky Move , Finucane and Smith, Lucy Guerin Company, Belvoir, Circus Oz and numerous productions at Malthouse Melbourne. She is also an artist at the performance company The Association of Optimism.

Verity Hampson
Lighting Designer

Verity graduated from NIDA in 2005. Previously she had specialised in corporate theatre design and technical management. Since 2005 she has worked extensively as a lighting, projection and set designer both in Australia and overseas in a range of performance styles including theatre, dance and Opera. Verity regularly works with the Griffin Theatre Company, her past productions at Griffin include *Angela's Kitchen*, *The Boys*, *This Year's Ashes*, *And No More Shall We Part*, *The Brothers Size*, *Like a Fishbone*, *Way to Heaven*, *Crestfall*, *References to Salvador Dali Make Me Hot*, *Dealing with Clair*, *Family Stories Belgrade*, *The Cold Child*, and *Live Acts on Stage*. She has collaborated with Lee Lewis on several projects including *That Face* for Company B in 2010. Verity has been a lighting director for the ABC's Live at The Basement, she also teaches the lighting design course at the National Institute of Dramatic Art. Verity is a recipient of the 2012 Mike Walsh Fellowship which she will spend working along side world renowned projection designers 59 Productions on a project at the Metropolitan Opera in New York. Her portfolio can be viewed at www.verityhampson.com.

Steve Francis
Composer and Sound Designer

Steve is a composer and sound designer who has worked extensively in theatre, dance and screen. His past productions for Griffin are *Between Two Waves*, *This Year's Ashes*, *Speaking in Tongues* and *Strange Attractor*. His other theatre credits include *The Secret River*, *Other Desert Cities*, *Sex with Strangers*, *The Splinter*, *Under Milk Wood*, *Les Liaisons Dangereuses*, *Pygmalion*, *Bloodland*, *Blood Wedding*, *The White Guard*, *Spring Awakening*, *The Removalists*, *Tusk Tusk*, *Gallipoli*, *The Great*, *Rabbit*, *Pig Iron People*, *Romeo and Juliet*, *The Taming of the Shrew*, *Embers*, *The 7 Stages of Grieving* and *Stolen* for Sydney Theatre Company. For Belvoir *Babyteeth*, *The Book of Everything*, *Gethsemane*, *The Power of Yes*, *Ruben Guthrie*, *Baghdad Wedding*, *Keating!*, *Paul*, *Parramatta Girls*, *Capricornia*, *The Spook*, *Box the Pony*, *Gulpilil* and *Page 8*. For dance, Steve has composed music for

Belong, *True Stories*, *Skin*, *Corroboree*, *Walkabout*, *Bush and Boomerang* (Bangarra Dance Theatre) and *Totem* (The Australian Ballet). His recent compositions for the screen include music for *Cops L.A.C.* for Channel 9, the Fox mini-series *Dangerous* and the short films *She Say*, *Dik* and *The Burnt Cork*. His awards include the 2012 Helpmann Award for *Belong* and 2003 Helpmann Awards for Best Original Score and Best New Australian Work for *Walkabout* and a 2011 Sydney Theatre Award for *The White Guard*.

Silvia Colloca
Performer

Born in Italy, Silvia Colloca first came to prominence as Dracula's Queen Bride in the feature film *Van Helsing* alongside Hugh Jackman. She went on to co-star in *The Detonator* opposite Wesley Snipes, in David Leland's *Virgin Territory* alongside Tim Roth, and in the camp classic *Vampire Killers* for legendary UK producer Steve Clark-Hall. Silvia's Australian feature film credits include Aaron Wilson's *Triple Happiness* and Sebastien Guy's *Nerve*. Silvia's television credits include guest roles in the ABC's acclaimed series *Rake* starring Richard Roxburgh, Packed to the Rafters and Cops LAC. Prior to these productions Silvia appeared as a series regular in the Italian television series *L'avvocato*. Silvia is a trained opera singer having graduated from the Scuola Musicale in Milan. Throughout 2008 and 2009 Silvia toured the United Kingdom with *Night at the Opera* which played at the iconic London Palladium, and accompanied virtuoso violinist David Garrett in his German *Encore* tour, and more recently sang the role of Orfeo in the Italian opera *Orfeo Ed Euridice* at the Pact Space in Sydney. In 2012 Silvia appeared in Aaron Wilson's feature film, *Triple Happiness*, and *Blood Wedding* for the Malthouse Theatre.

Matt Zeremes
Performer

Matt graduated from the Queensland University of Technology with a Bachelor of Fine Arts (Acting). Matt achieved public and critical acclaim in the world-premiere production of *Holding the Man* for Griffin Theatre Company. He enjoyed five additional seasons, clocking in over 300 shows at Griffin, Sydney Opera House, Belvoir, Brisbane Powerhouse and Melbourne Theatre Company. This show marked his London West End debut in 2010. Matt is currently in post-production on his new feature film—*SuperAwesome!* He has written, directed, produced and starred in two other feature films. His first—*Burke and Wills* had its world premiere at the Tribeca Film Festival before being theatrically released throughout Australia. Matt's second feature film *Strangers Lovers Killers* has been sold internationally. Matt's television work includes, *Underbelly, Home and Away, Chandon Pictures, All Saints, The Surgeon, Firestorm, Small Claims 2, Fatal Honeymoon* which starred Harvey Keitel for the Lifetime channel in the US and most recently he featured in *The Elegant Gentlemen's Guide to Knife Fighting* for the ABC. Matt's other feature film work includes *All My Friends are Leaving Brisbane, Solo, Circle of Lies* and the soon to be released *Aim High in Creation*. Stage credits include *Embers, Saturn's Return* (Sydney Theatre Company), *Becky Shaw* (Ensemble Theatre), *10,000 Beers* (Darlinghurst Theatre), *Jesus Hopped the A-Train* (B-Sharp). Matt has also staged six independent shows himself, including the Sydney premiere of Kenneth Lonnergan's *This is Our Youth* and the Australian premiere of *Tiny Dynamite*, both awarded best independent production of the year. Other plays include *Little Malcolm and His Struggle Against the Eunuchs*, and *Ninja*. Matt is a proud member of MEAA.

Karina McKenzie
Stage Manager

Karina has been working as a freelance event and stage manager in Melbourne and Sydney since graduating from Theatre/Media at CSU. Past productions include: Helpmann awarding winning *Angela's Kitchen* (2010, 2012) and *Strange Attractor* (Griffin Theatre Company), *Boxing Day* (Critical Stages), *Bear Hunt, My Wonderful Day, Halpern and Johnson, Ninety* (Ensemble Theatre Company), *RU4Me* (True West Productions), *Transparency* (Seymour Centre and Riverside Production), *La Sonnambula* (Pacific Opera), *The Knowing of Mary Poppins* (Darlinghurst Theatre Company), *The Taming of the Shrew, Richard III, The Wind in the Willows* (Australian Shakespeare Company). She also works on events across Sydney including the Sydney Writers' Festival and St. George OpenAir Cinema.

LAVENDER CUPCAKES WITH HONEY FROSTING

Method

Cream together butter and sugar. Add eggs, then flour, milk and lavender. Beat to a smooth batter. Bake in preheated (180 degrees) oven as follows:

For cupcakes (18-24), bake 20-25 mins

In a 20cm round cake tin, bake 55 mins

In a 22cm round cake tin, bake 40 mins

Cake is cooked when golden brown on top and a butter knife comes out clean.

Using electric beaters, cream the butter until it is very pale and fluffy. Add the icing sugar and continue to beat. Add the milk, a little at a time, until the icing is a good consistency (it needs to be firm enough to create a thick layer but not so thick that it breaks the crust off the cake as you spread it on).

For Cupcakes

Mix the honey in with the icing and spread on cooled cupcakes. To frost cupcakes neatly, get a little frosting on a butter knife and smear it right in the middle of the cupcake. Turn the cupcake around in your hand as you spread the icing out toward the edges of the cake. This way you won't get icing all over the edge of the patty pans, which detracts from the look of the cupcakes considerably - and isn't the adorableness of cupcakes half the fun? Top with a fresh lavender flower to serve.

Courtesy of Jess Moore

Ingredients

125g butter, softened

3/4 cup castor sugar

2 eggs

1 1/2 cups self-raising flour

1/2 cup milk

pinch bicarb soda

1 1/2 tbsp lavender

200g butter, softened

4 cups icing sugar

1-2 tbsp honey

1/4 cup milk

red and blue food colouring, OR fresh lavender flowers

ABOUT GRIFFIN

Griffin Theatre Company is Australia's only new writing theatre. In residence at Sydney's historic SBW Stables Theatre, we lead the country in developing and producing great Australian stories, and are dedicated to supporting Australian artists.

For over 30 years we've been dedicated to bringing audiences the highest standards of theatrical craft and the most unforgettable Australian plays. Australia's most loved and performed play – Michael Gow's *Away* – premiered at Griffin. The hit films *Lantana* and *The Boys* also began life as plays first produced by the company, as did the TV series *Heartbreak High*.

We also have a passion for developing Australian talent, with many of our nation's most celebrated artists starting their professional careers here.

Griffin produces an annual subscription season of four to five main stage shows by Australian playwrights, and co-presents a season of new work with our leading independent artists. We also support artists through professional development opportunities, including artist residencies and masterclasses.

The SBW Stables provides an experience like no other – up close and personal for actors and audiences. It's Sydney's most intimate and persuasive stage.

Griffin Theatre Company
13 Craigend St
Kings Cross NSW 2011

Phone 02 9332 1052

Fax 02 9331 1524

Email info@griffintheatre.com.au

Web www.griffintheatre.com.au

SBW Stables Theatre
10 Nimrod St
Kings Cross NSW 2011

Online bookings at
griffintheatre.com.au
or call 02 9361 3817

H⊛tHouse

GREAT AUSTRALIAN THEATRE RIGHT ON YOUR DOORSTEP

HotHouse is a producer, a presenter and an incubator of contemporary Australian theatre. It has been at the forefront of theatre practice since 1997 and is a regional company renowned nationally as a centre of excellence for the development and presentation of new work.

HotHouse commissions from leading Australian playwrights annually and facilitates the very popular and highly successful 'artists in residence' development program, *A Month in the Country*, in partnership with Albury City. Since its inception in 2004, *A Month in the Country* has hosted over 400 artists (writers, designers, dancers, musicians, composers, video artists, choreographers, circus artists and physical theatre performers) and added over 40 new works to the Australian canon.

HotHouse operates the Butter Factory Theatre on Gateway Island in the Murray River – and like the river that surrounds it, HotHouse nourishes and nurtures – specifically the development and growth of new Australian theatre.

HotHouse gratefully acknowledges the support of The Besen Family Foundation and the Pierce Armstrong Foundation.

ABOUT
MERRIGONG THEATRE COMPANY

Merrigong Theatre Company manages one of Australia's busiest, most dynamic regional venues - Illawarra Performing Arts Centre in Wollongong, about an hour south of Sydney. Merrigong is also a vibrant theatre company in its own right - producing, presenting and touring exciting contemporary theatre and supporting the development of a diverse range of independent theatre-makers.

Merrigong presents a diverse annual season of theatre, dance and children's programming. Our theatre and dance subscription packages include work sourced from Australia's finest performing arts companies (such as Sydney Theatre Company and Bangarra Dance Theatre), self-produced work, acclaimed international productions, and innovative contemporary work from new companies.

Through the **Make It @Merrigong** program, Merrigong is committed to commissioning and developing new Australian works for future productions, and supporting the development and presentation of the work of local independent artists through new and established performance platforms and regular development opportunities.

In 2006, Merrigong began producing full-scale productions in-house. Since then, Merrigong productions have included Van Badham's *Camarilla* (2006), Athol Fugard's *Valley Song* (2007), Marcel Dorney's *Thieves Like Us* (2008) and *Charcoal Creek* (2012), Caleb Lewis' *Death in Bowengabbie* (2010), Mary Rachel Brown's *The Dapto Chaser* (2011) and Alana Valentine's *Dead Man Brake* (2013). Merrigong co-productions include *The Table of Knowledge* (2011), produced with acclaimed Sydney-based company version 1.0, and *The Bull, the Moon and the Coronet of Stars* (2013) with Griffin Theatre Company and Hothouse Theatre.

Merrigong Theatre Company at Illawarra Performing Arts Centre

32 Burelli Street, Wollongong NSW 2500

Phone 02 4224 5999
Fax 02 4226 9696
Email info@merrigong.com.au
Web www.merrigong.com.au

Merrigong Staff

ARTISTIC DIRECTOR / CEO
Simon Hinton

Assistant to the Artistic Director / CEO
Rachel Dyer

PRODUCTION AND TECHNICAL MANAGER
Michael Gill

Technical Co-ordinator
James Clarke

Technical Co-ordinator
Warwick Mann

Operations Co-ordinator
Steven Robinson

MARKETING MANAGER
Edie Watt

Education and Media Co-ordinator
Jennifer O'Sullivan

Marketing Co-ordinator
Candice Greenwood

FINANCE AND BUSINESS MANAGER
Judi Douglas

Finance Assistant
Heike Obermayr

Venue and Front of House Co-ordinator
Gia Frino

ARTISTIC ASSOCIATE
Anne-Louise Rentell

Artistic & Community Projects Co-ordinator
Clare Spillman

Regional Outreach Co-ordinator
Lilli Pang

BOX OFFICE MANAGER
Linda Hanbury

Box Office Assistant
Evelyn Andrews

Merrigong would like to thank the following funding partners and sponsors:

wollongong city of innovation | Wollongong City Council is the major funding partner of Merrigong Theatre Co. | NSW Trade & Investment Arts NSW | MERCURY | 96.5 WAVE FM | 2ST | PRiME7 | Adina apartment hotels

GRIFFIN STAFF AND DONORS

Income from Griffin activities covers less than 50% of our operating costs – leaving an ever increasing gap for us to fill through government funding sponsorship and the generosity of our individual supporters. Your support helps us bridge the gap and keep ticket prices affordable and our work at its best. To make a donation and a difference, contact Griffin on 9332 1052 or donate online at griffintheatre.com.au.

Commission $12,500+
Darin-Cooper family
Anthony and Suzanne Maple-Brown

Production $10,000+
Anonymous (2)
Estate of the late Ruth Barratt
Sophie McCarthy & Antony Green

Studio $5,000
Gil Appleton
Alex Byrne & Sue Hearn
James Emmett & Peter Wilson
Ros & Paul Espie
Fiona Garrood, Matthew May
& Ayumu Kaneda
The Goodness Foundation
Limb Family Foundation
Richard & Elizabeth Longes
Rhonda McIver
Leigh O'Neill
Geoff & Wendy Simpson

Workshop $1,000-$4,999
Dr Gae Anderson
Baly Douglass Foundation
Daniel Brezniak
Richard Cottrell
Innes Ferguson
Peter Graves
Larry & Tina Grumley
John & Mary Holt
Ken & Lilian Horler
Margaret Johnston
Stephen Manning
Peter & Diane O'Connell
Stuart Thomas
Estate of the late
Leslie N Walford
Paul & Jennifer Winch

Reading $500-$999
Anonymous (3)
Jes Andersen
Wendy Ashton
Jason Bourne
Alex Bowen & Catherine Sullivan
Angela Bowne
Michael & Colleen Chesterman
Wendy Elder
Elizabeth Evatt
Jono Gavin
Peter & Rosemary Ingle

Alexandra Joel & Philip Mason
Henry Johnston
Dr Stephen McNamara
Dr David Nguyen
Lynne O'Neill
Anthony Paull
Natalie Pelham
Annabel Ritchie
Lesley & Andrew Rosenberg
Isla Tooth
Vodafone Foundation
Louise Walsh & Dave Jordan
Dr Bill Winspear

First Draft $200-$499
Anonymous (4)
Jane Bridge
Katharine Brisbane
Rob Brookman
Corinne Campbell & Bryan Everts
Victor Cohen & Rosie McColl
Bryony & Timothy Cox
Max Dingle
Eric Dole
Peter Fritz
Gadens Lawyers
Julien & Monica Ginsberg
Brenda Gottsche
Janet Heffernan
Danielle Hoareau
Beverley Johnson
Lou Lander
Jennifer Ledgar & Bob Lim
Christopher McCabe
Duncan McKay
Sarah Miller
Neville Mitchell
Philip & Monica Moore
Alex-Oonagh Redmond
Catherine Rothery
Diane & David Russell
Michelle Shek
Ross Steele
Ros Tarszisz
Jane Thorn

We would also like to thank
Peter O'Connell and Jon Clark
for their expertise, guidance
and time.

Current as of 06 March 2013

GRIFFIN SPONSORS

Griffin would like to thank the following:

Government Supporters

Australian Government | Australia Council for the Arts | Trade & Investment Arts NSW | CITY OF SYDNEY

Patron

SBW Foundation — SEABORN, BROUGHTON & WALFORD FOUNDATION

2013 Season Sponsor

Interbrand

Production Sponsors

HOLDING REDLICH · nabprivatewealth · nab

Associate Sponsors

MARQUE · tonkin zulaikha greer ARCHITECTS · OTTO RISTORANTE · BDO

Company Sponsors

WHIRLWIND — More than ink on paper · V & R THE VICTORIA ROOM BAR RESTAURANT · EIGHT HOTELS AUSTRALIA Boutique Hotel Collection · CURRENCY PRESS

Time Out Sydney timeout.com/sydney · bourke street bakery · Rosenfeld, Kant & Co. Business & Financial Solutions

SIGNWAVE NEWTOWN · MOPPITY Vineyards

UNSW THE UNIVERSITY OF NEW SOUTH WALES · goget.com.au · REGENTS COURT UNIQUE STYLISH STUDIO ACCOMMODATION

Foundations and Trusts

MALCOLM ROBERTSON FOUNDATION · CAL Cultural Fund · GIRGENSOHN FOUNDATION · ROBERTSON FOUNDATION

Griffin Theatre Company is assisted by the Australian Government through the Australia Council, its arts funding and advisory body; and the NSW Government through Arts NSW.

www.ingramcontent.com/pod-product-compliance
Lightning Source LLC
Chambersburg PA
CBHW041934090426
42744CB00017B/2058